ZERO TO SIXTY (PAGES)

SELECTED VIGNETTES

FROM THE BOOK:

"TRAX

WE MADE IN

NEW YORK

1968-72

Volume 1"

ALISTAIR RAPIDS PUBLISHING INC.

GRAND RAPIDS, MICHIGAN

This little book (ZERO TO SIXTY)
consists exclusively of selected portions of
TRAX WE MADE IN NEW YORK 1968-72 Volume 1,
and is designed to serve as an introduction
to the upcoming TRAX Instruction Manual.

This new manual will fully equip readers
to conceive of, create and record
their own sets of personal history, and do so
in the most exciting and simple method possible.
Keep a watchful eye open for the
TRAX Instruction Manual.

"COMPARATIVE PNEMONICS"

"When I was younger, I could remember anything, whether it
happened or not." — Mark Twain

Published 2025 by Alistair Rapids Publishing, Grand Rapids, MI.

ISBN: 978-1-936092-24-6 (trade pbk) 1-936092-25-3 Kindle E-Book
Printed in the United States of America

Library of Congress Cataloging-in-Publication Data

Carrier, Michael, and Carrier, Evie.

TRAX—ZERO TO SIXTY (PAGES) IN MINUTES/ by Michael Carrier and Evie Carrier. ISBN: 978-1-936092-25-6 (trade pbk. : alk. paper)
1. Autobiography 2. Memoir 3. Comparative Mnemonics 4. New York.

Vignette 1—Evie's First Visit to New York

According to Boy: Ten bucks seemed like an awful lot of money to me. as I didn't have a real job—I was a graduate fellow at NYU (At least that's what I called myself. I had a "National Defence Education Act Title IV Fellowship". The stipend I received covered food and lodging, but that was about all. I am not sure what indentured servitude might feel like, but I think my first year at NYU gave me a hint.

The bus ride from the East Side Air Terminal (which might have been Grand Central Terminal) to LaGuardia cost ten dollars. It would be times three—one fare got me to the airport, then two fares got the two of us back to Manhattan. Then there would be three more fares for the return trip. Sixty bucks, plus subway fare from my apartment to the Air Terminal, plus cab fare from the Air Terminal back to the apartment after I had picked Evie up at LaGuardia.

I had planned to take the subway from the apartment to the Air Terminal, but I would not put Evie on a subway with her luggage.

I had a whole list of subway rules. One of them was, "Never ride the subway carrying anything that was not a weapon, could not be used as a weapon, or was too precious to leave behind." If I rode the subway, I always wanted to be able to run in case of trouble. I was an excellent runner—five miles twice a day. I figured it was smarter, and safer, to run away from trouble than to confront it.

Another subway rule was never to sit down. It's just too hard to escape from that position. Also, I never liked to ride the subway with anyone for whom I was responsible. I always believed I could escape a conflict, but the odds against avoiding danger diminished when there were additional people to protect.

For the most part, my subway rules applied only after dark, not during rush hours. Rush hours were pretty safe, I thought. But if I wanted to go to a club or a restaurant at night, I hailed a cab.

I took a subway this night because I could dress down to quasi street person level. That made me feel safe—I didn't look like I even had subway fare. And, I wanted to save money.

"Sometimes a little paranoia is just good thinking," I always thought and frequently said.

I was so looking forward to seeing her. Even though I was mentally complaining about the cost of airport transportation, I would have gladly sold my car (if I had one) to cover the cost. For the first time in my life I loved someone more than I loved myself. I was crazy about her. Her lips were soft and kissable. They had an unbelievably sweet taste, and I am not talking about her lipstick, or her Estee Lauder Youth Dew perfume. When we kissed, her lips, or perhaps her breath, had a hot sweetness. I was captivated by that taste 24/7. I could think of nothing else.

I had not seen her for over a month. It was horrible. It was like nothing I had ever before imagined. Food didn't even taste good. All I could do is think about her.

She was tall, by most standards—five feet, six and a half inches. I think she appeared even taller because she was very trim. Not skinny, though—her butt was full, and her legs perfectly shaped.

She enhanced her aura of tallness by wearing high-heeled footwear—high-heeled boots, high-heeled clogs, and just plain high-heeled shoes.

And she was good at wearing high heels. "Elegant" is the best word I can think of to describe her. Not even a hint of awkwardness. I had never seen a woman handle herself as well as she did in high heels. That thought alone could keep me up nights.

Her face was beautiful, with high cheek bones. She liked to think of herself as an Audrey Hepburn "Sabrina" in Paris. And I think that she did have that look. I think she liked to identify with the Hepburn's character.

But, I thought of her more as an Ava Gardner. I just hoped she would never find a Spanish bullfighter and leave me high and dry like Ava did Frank.

Anyway, I always thought Ava was the most beautiful woman to have walked the face of the earth, and I was in love with her younger look alike, Evie.

Then, as now, I loved her more than anything else in this life.

Evie's first visit to New York according to Girl: United Airlines was happy to have me on that big silver bird that day, I was so very excited to be leaving the great state of Michigan, with the lake effect overcast days, and endless waves of clouds and dreariness.

My mind raced as I realized that I was about to take off. Back in the 60s the stewardesses were nice, they were impeccably dressed, nails painted, with sparkling white teeth behind their Miss America smiles. They were there to offer me tea, coffee, donuts or whatever my heart desired.

It did not matter what they were offering because my heart desired someone 700 miles away in New York. I could picture him waiting for me to get off that plane. As the jets started their typical noisy winding up, my heart was winding up as well. I sat back in my seat. I am sure I had a big smile on my face, as I allowed the rush of the runway takeoff to take my breath away. I was ecstatic. First the front of the plane lifted off, then the rear. As the plane continued to climb to the top of the clouds I felt my heart lose touch with the mundane of Michigan. I was ready to start a new adventure.

Mom and Dad were wonderful parents, but when I got to be 20ish, I knew it was time to make my own life. I packed lightly, because I did not want to have to explain where I was going. I parked my 1965 buttercup yellow mustang at the airport, pulled out my bag, wearing the brown boots that matched my medium length "unstyled" brown hair, denim jacket, and all of the mascara and eyeliner that I could possibly put on. That was my style. I knew that New York and I would hit it off just fine. It was, after all, the days of flower children—happy little kids, not wanting to quite grow up, but, wanting all of the fun that grownups have. That defined me pretty well.

The two hour trip from Grand Rapids to LaGuardia went much too slowly for me. I needed to see my guy. He was so very intriguing—a brilliant scholar, and very cute. And, he was from South Haven (Michigan). I remembered that an acquaintance had once told me that South Haven is known for really cute guys—and she was right. Mike was tan, tall and handsome. He was very opinionated. He knew what he liked, and what he didn't like. He could discuss politics, good books, writing, religion, and he had a lot of just practical knowledge. Once he even took the plumbing apart at a hotel just to retrieve my contacts (but that's another story).

Mike and I just hit it off. He could make me laugh. We could sit by each other for hours and not say a word. We liked the same things—corny movies, popcorn, pizza, Perry Mason, and just about everything else.

We had been writing feverishly back and forth for the past year. Sometimes the letters were goofy, sometimes they were serious; but they were all "really missing you" letters.

It was a long year to be away from each other. The days of undergraduate school were gone for both of us—I had spent the past year working third shift in a factory, and Mike had been granted a graduate fellowship to attend New York University.

I liked to work, but that job did not excite me. The company I worked for did send me to soldering school. When I finished my training my first job was soldering circuit boards for the landing gear on Lear jets. Wisely, when my supervisor discovered that too many of my soldering joints were a mess, he transferred me to a clean room, third shift, no supervision, welding and sandblasting under a microscope.

It was nice to be trusted and on my own; however, I did not want to spend the rest of my life there. Most of the other women in the factory were wrinkled smokers, divorced and unhappy. Their life at the bar after work was all they got up for. That was not for me. So I worked hard, saved money, and put in my time thinking about a better future. I would take my entire lunch and break time to compose almost a letter a night to my love. I would even paint flowers or hearts and decorate the envelope, using pink and green markers and ink to make that girly statement. Mike loved it, even if the post office and mailman found it hard to decipher where to deliver my letters.

With my memories of the past year whirling through my mind, all of a sudden I felt the plane descend. "Oh my gosh, it won't be long now." The stewardess (now known as a "flight attendant") reminded us all to get back to our seats and make sure our seatbelts were buckled, because we would be landing in twenty minutes. The plane was slowing down and from my window seat (I have always liked the windows) I could see the skyline of New York, the Empire State Building, Yankee Stadium, and Central Park. There was no World Trade Center yet; but the granite and concrete of that big rock called Manhattan was getting closer.

LaGuardia, I later learned, was actually in Queens. I did not understand all the intricacies associated with the five-borough concept, the islands that made up the city, the government, the politics, the laws, the dangers or the wonderful ethnicity of this great city. I did not even notice that the landing approach at LaGuardia airport was built out over the water. And as I look back, it did not even worry me that it looked like we would be piloted into the drink. Nope, I was trying to picture what his expression would be when he first caught a glimpse of me.

The wonderful pilot landed the plane smoothly and we were allowed to exit the plane. Everyone was so very nice to me, probably because they could see I was in love and the world was a better place because of it. It seemed to me on that June day in 1968, nothing in the world could ever stop my determination to find my guy and follow my dream.

There was a line of people waiting for their loved ones. I looked for his green eyes and incredible smile when I got off the plane, but could not find him. I followed the signs to the escalator, and headed down. It was then that I saw him. There he stood at the very bottom, flashing his incredible smile and sparkly eyes. I am sure he had all this planned. He probably walked around looking for the most dramatic place to meet me. I knew when our eyes met, that our lives would from this point on be different—different and better.

If I had any doubts before, they were now gone. As our eyes met that day at LaGuardia, I knew we were both ready for a commitment, and that we both wanted to spend our time together—not 700 miles apart.

The real skinny (according to Boy): As usual, Evie got some things right, and some wrong. One thing she got entirely right was her exuberance about traveling to New York. She was excited. However, in the forty plus years we have been married, I could count on one hand (not counting thumb or pinky) the number of times I have ever seen her not at the top of her game. She is an incredibly happy person. She has truly made my life wonderful. To this day, when we get in the car to head to the airport for a trip, she puts her emotions into a higher gear. She is a joy to travel with.

Of course, she was correct when she wrote that I was a "cute guy"; but she was wrong when she referred to me as a "brilliant scholar." That was just not the case. I was a very good student, but not a brilliant scholar—the two are very different. I suppose you could say I had her fooled a little bit.

I'm glad I was the one who drew the task of writing the "Real Skinny" on her first trip to New York. I think I have read her take on it five times tonight—I'm getting really excited.

And, she is right about a couple more things. I am sure I was smiling when I looked at her at the top of the escalator. I doubt that I have ever been able to look at her without smiling. And, I did arrive at the airport early enough to find the best place to greet her. I wanted to watch her descend to me. It was magic.

Vignette 2—New York accommodations when Evie came to visit

According to Boy: I was never able to understand why hotels such as the Statler Hilton and the Waldorf-Astoria gave me a discount when I rented a room. To me that did not make any sense. The way I figured, it was a lot like a bar discounting the price of sandwiches for non-drinkers. Why? A hotel should cater to a clientele that has money to spend in its restaurants, gift shops and bars—that would not be students. Also, I suspect that students (in 1968) bounced a higher percentage of checks than business travelers. And if anyone was going to steal a robe or a towel, or tear up the place, I'd bet it would more likely be the student, than the family man. So why give lowly students a discount? Beats me. I guess I will have to defer to Hilary Bradt on that one. Nevertheless, I asked for a student discount, and they gave me one.

I am not exactly sure what it cost to spend a night at the Waldorf, but sixty-five dollars per night sounds right. While coming up with that amount was not an insurmountable task, it did require me to save up. I did not have a credit card, so I would have to pay cash up front. Who knows what would have happened had I run up a lot of additional expenses? I think that there might not have been a charge for local calls, and the only way to place a long distance one was "collect." So there really wasn't much of a way to run up charges.

Evie's contact lenses always presented a challenge. We literally spent almost the whole time in bed. What an adventure that was. She was so incredibly fun to make love with. How very crazy it is to be so very much in love, and not have to get out of bed to go to work—at least for a few days. We usually bought the use of the room for three nights. That's about all we could afford, and about all the time we could take off. So, what's the deal about Evie's contacts?

Within the first fifteen minutes after arriving at the hotel, Evie would take out her contacts, and place them in a hotel glass, on the back of the bathroom sink, with about two ounces of water. We would then make love the rest of the night, and wake up about noon the next day.

Of course, the first thing I did, upon waking up, was always to brush my teeth, or get a drink of water.

Not yet familiar with Evie's habit of leaving her contact lenses submerged in a glass of water on the back of the sink, on this one occasion I grabbed a glass from the back of the sink. Noticing that it had a little stale water in it, I dumped it out, and ran fresh water in it.

Later, when Evie got up, she asked me if I had seen a partial glass of water with her contacts on the bottom of it.

"I think I know where they might be," I told her.

Using only my hands, with a damp washcloth to provide a better grip, I disassembled the plumbing. I engaged the stopper in the sink, and dumped the horrible-smelling dregs from the trap into the sink. Carefully I examined every tiny piece of debris until I found the first contact. I had locked the bathroom door so Evie would not have to suffer the odor, nor view the mess I was making. I placed the filthy contact back in the glass, and went after the other one. Eventually I found the second one, and put it with its buddy in the glass. I ran a little water on them to keep them moist. I was pretty proud of myself, but I still was not ready to return them to Evie.

I then put the sink back together, and washed the stinking black mess down the drain. I scrubbed my hands well with bar soap, and then cleaned the contacts as best I could.

Eventually I unlocked the door and invited Evie in to see what I had found. "How did you find them?" She asked me, visibly shocked to discover that I had located her contacts.

"You really don't want to learn the details," I told her. "Just be sure to clean them well before you put them in."

This same thing happed a few months later at another hotel. This time, however, I was unable to find the contacts. In fact, I remembered drinking the water in the glass, and probably ingesting those miniature Frisbees.

It seemed so amazing to me that I could totally mess up her vision like that, and she never spoke a cross word to me. I recall thinking that this girl must be an angel, or else she really loved me. As it turned out, both were true.

N ew York accommodations when Evie came to visit according to Girl: Just like little Annie Oakley, when I came to town I was "packing." However, I was not packing a 22 caliber rifle (to split a playing card edge on, and put five or six more holes in it before it hit the ground).

What I packed were two main ingredients for a trip to see Mike. First, of course, my birth control pills, yep, this little sharpshooter did not need to return to Michigan with a problem. And, secondly, my contact lenses.

Didn't need a suitcase for those. Didn't have to check a bag at the airport. I could wear Mike's shirts for my sleepwear and after two quick days for a visit, I would be back in the Midwest.

They would be impromptu, I would call Mike and tell him I needed to see him. My check would come, I would head to the bank to cash it. I then went to the airport and bought my ticket. And, by the next weekend, I was in flight.

I can't believe we could smoke on the plane. No screening, no IDs—

anyone with a ticket could get on a plane. The planes were big and loud. I think that the sky would shake when those silver bullets careened through the clouds. The flight attendants were all girls. Not a hair out of place, nails with clear polish and white pearly teeth showed when the red lips parted to offer drinks or dinner. The visits were fast and incredibly delicious. When there was a roommate involved, we would head to the Statler Hilton and get the student rate rooms.

It was there I lost my, no, not lost, I misplaced, no, perhaps the glass of water should have been less available. But, the contacts were gone in the morning. My view of Manhattan was suddenly diminished. The Staten Island Ferry would not have the clear view of the city, the Empire State Building would wait for another weekend. Sites would wait. It was okay because we could spend more face time.

We imagined they were down the drain. Yes, with the slimiest of sewer rats. They would probably be taking them to the rat pawn shop at the entrance to the train tunnel. The finder would discuss their value with the owner, and they decided to re-sell them as glass bowls, hand-made, each being unique, and the little artist's mark in the right lens to determined authenticity, much like the digital watermarking software used for a photograph.

So, the little rat family, had a fabulous dinner with the pawnbrokers bounty, and I jumped on the Sunday night plane, a bit blinder, but, with the Annie song running through my mind.

"Buffalo gals, won't you come out tonight?

Come out tonight, Come out tonight?

Buffalo gals, won't you come out tonight,

And dance by the light of the moon."

(by Cool White, copyright unknown; featured in *It's A Wonderful Life*.)

And as for me—I will be back. Within a few weeks I will be packin', just watch me.

The real skinny (according to Boy): So often, when I think about Evie, I am reminded of the movie, *My Cousin Vinny*. The movie was made in 1992, and starred Joe Pesci and the second cutest girl in the world, Marisa Tomei. I would be hard pressed to describe my favorite scene—they are all great. But the one I recall best is the one where Vinny presses a witness (Vinny was a trial lawyer) to state how cute his girlfriend was. That's how I have always viewed Evie. She's cute.

Not only is she cute, but she is a darn good writer. Don't you just love her little rat story? I wish I had thought of that. She doesn't, however, mention the fact that one time I was able to retrieve her contacts from the drain. There would have been no point trying the second time, because I knew exactly where they were. I will concede the fact that they might eventually have ended up in that rat pawn shop (more than likely, however, via the East River).

Vignette 3—Christmas party at Water Lift

According to Boy: This episode took place after I had moved to New York, but before we got married. It would have been the Christmas of 1967, the same Christmas I bought the huge orange and red throw rug for Evie. We had two big events planned for the few days I was to be in Grand Rapids, one was Christmas dinner at my brother George's house, and the other was the annual Christmas party at Water Lift (the company where Evie worked).

I was scared to death at the prospect of being interrogated by all of Evie's friends, and I suspect she was equally intimidated at the thought of meeting my whole family. It would have been so much more fun had Evie simply flown out to New York, and we could have had a great time by ourselves at Rockefeller Center and Times Square.

I had no notion as to what to expect. What if her girlfriends at Water Lift were like the chick cliques in high school? All that note passing and speaking in code. What if one of her guy friends were to have had a thing for her? That could be uncomfortable. I was not looking forward to the party.

Being the Olympic-sized coward that I tend to be when drastically out of my element, I shopped around at the local liquor stores until I found a bottle of 151 proof Demerara Rum. My reasoning was, no matter how badly the night went, the Demerara Rum could erase it from my memory. But, like most events in life, the anxiety and dread beforehand are almost never mirrored by the actual event.

When we got there, I do recall having a swig of the rum, then a second, and then a third. My head started to feel the power of the alcohol. We then went in.

I don't remember much about the night. I recall meeting some really nice people. Without exception the comment I heard when I was introduced was: "So you're the guy from New York…" It was very obvious that all of Evie's friends had a lot of respect for her.

I actually started having a good time. I could be wrong, but I think we danced almost every dance—and I did not know how to dance.

"It's easy. Nothing to it," Evie told me, grabbing me by the hand and pulling me on the dance floor every time the band played a Polka.

I knew better than to mix the types of alcohol I was drinking, so I found the rum at the bar. There is no doubt that I was drinking too much. My head was ringing; but we kept dancing.

We kept dancing that night until we stopped dancing, and the "stop" was sudden. I have no idea how they expected us to dance around the huge steel supports that held up the roof of the hall. Initially I was able to miss them. After a time—after too many dances and many too many rums—I slammed Evie into one of the posts.

"Bam." Her whole torso struck it at once. I felt the impact on her body. It did not knock her out, but it was certainly must have been close.

"Maybe we should sit the rest of this out," I said, helping her back to our table. She never complained about it, but I am sure she developed some serious bruising as a result. A short time later we excused ourselves and left.

As I reflect on that evening, three or four things come to mind. First, I was amazed to learn how good a dancer Evie was. While my lack of ability in that area surely diminished our performance together, it did not cloud my ability to appreciate her dancing. Second, I was very impressed at the quality of those she considered her friends, and how they admired her. Third, I really liked the way she treated me that night. I felt really good just being with her. And, finally, I really liked the way her body felt when I held her. We had caressed before, and kissed; but, the magic of her body moving to the music, in my arms, was beyond amazing. Its memory makes me warm to this day.

Christmas party at Water Lift according to Girl: Water Lift—new job, new dress, awesome party, splendid date. It began with soldering school that spring. I went to classes for a week. Driving back and forth to Kalamazoo every day with a very tall girl, Jillian, who was hired in the same week. We thought it would be easier to share the driving responsibilities and gas. She had graduated a year ahead of me from Creston High School (home of the Polar Bears). She was pretty, and very tall—over six feet. She could have been a model, or a dancer. But she, as did I, found the help wanted ad in the paper that previous weekend and chose to work in a "clean" factory environment, wearing jeans and sweatshirts, as opposed to working on a semi-assembly line. It was one huge room, big enough to park a few planes inside, with partitioned cubbies for the managers. We had twelve foot tables put together and had three shifts working around the clock on the latest project—the winning bids from the airline industry. The tables were filled with gray plastic bins, much like a busboy would use to clear a table, and the bins were filled with green circuit boards of all sizes and shapes. The object of the game was to find the right transistor, diode, or resistor with the correct colors and twist and bend the wires to fit in the teeny holes, then use a wire cutter, solder, and flux and present our foreman with the beginnings of a beautiful bouquet to grace the landing gear of a jet plane.

School didn't help, my soldering skills were zip. I hated it. The smell, smoke, burned fingers and worst of all, my rejects, did nothing for my self image. How could this be? I was never, ever really bad at anything. I tried harder, used more flux, less flux, hotter irons, quicker moves, but I just couldn't get past the inspectors. I wanted to do well, I tried everything I could think of, and it did not help. I was called into the office, we discussed job performance, and I was moved.

Fall came, and all the girls in the lunchroom were so excited. They were lighting up one cigarette after another as they talked. Sandwiches were left uneaten and chattering was at a deafening decibel level.

"Jillian, what's going on?"

Management had just posted news on the annual Christmas Party. It was to be held at a banquet hall, the company was providing the food, refreshments, dancing and entertainment. We could bring a date. Our tables filled with middle-aged women and young girls just out of high school, all were getting ideas for what to wear and who to bring.

"Mike, can you make it to my work Christmas Party?"

He said he wouldn't miss it, he would be in Grand Rapids on his school break, staying with his brother George, and we could go together.

My new dress was red, short, with eight big plastic buttons down the front (four on each side), with a black collar. I wore patent leather black boots with a black bag to match. My coat was black wool. It was short, with a belt of the same wool with a big silver buckle.

I had black gloves and a scarf to keep me warm on that cold December night.

We started the night out with introductions; Mike met tall Jillian, the girls from the line, and my boss, Larry, who was so kind when I got bumped off the soldering line.

We hit the drinks next.

The band played on.

We danced as lovers do—twirling in each other's arms. The world could have been watching us, but we did not know, it was just Mike and me.

I wanted it to be the two of us forever.

Once in a while, when getting on a plane these days, I wonder about the transistors. I wonder about the circuit boards that had passed through my hands. Some of those planes are decades old.

I shake myself and wake up.

 Impossible.

My stuff never passed. The world is safe.

Thank goodness.

The real skinny (according to Girl): One of the things I remember best about that Christmas was the present Mike brought me from New York—a hand woven wool throw rug (Chapter 79). It was amazing. I loved it. It was totally unexpected and beautiful. I wish we still had it, but after moving it a trillion times, it did not make the final "cut."

As far as the Christmas party at Water Lift was concerned—we did have a few drinks. That was very true. While I am positive that the party actually happened, it remains a big blur. The whole factory showed up, the tables were beautiful, the music divine, but Mike was not accustomed to the Polka, and I found myself stepping all over him. We laughed until we finally excused ourselves and "split that popsicle stand

Vignette 4—Railroads and cemeteries

According to Boy: Early on in our New York adventure, Evie's brother Tim called us and asked if he and a few of his friends could come out and visit us. We were immediately excited at the prospect. The only problem was, we did not have any idea where we should take them. We were very familiar with the city, but our interests were not tourist-type interests. Evie and I could have a good time just knocking around the Village; we didn't have any interest in taking sight-seeing trips. So, we decided to ask our landlords, the Robinsons.

Charlie Robinson Sr. suggested a number of places of interest to visitors. These included the old standbys such as the Statue of Liberty, Rockefeller Center, the Empire State Building, Wall Street, and Times Square. One of his most interesting suggestions was the Staten Island Ferry. "Hey, for a nickel you can take a really nice ride out to Staten Island. You can see the Statue of Liberty, and get a good view of the New York skyline."

The nickel part sounded good to me. I asked Charlie how much the Statue of Liberty tour cost, and he told me he didn't know. He called his wife, and asked her. She said she didn't know either. So I asked them how much it cost the last time they went. I was shocked to learn that neither of them had ever gone out to the island to see the Statue of Liberty.

"We've never seen the Statue, except from a distance," Charlie told me. "In fact, no one I know from the neighborhood has ever been out to the Statue."

"How about the Empire State Building?" I asked.

"Never."

"Times Square?"

"Yeah, we went there when we were dating."

That's when I realized that no one who lived in that part of Queens ever left Queens. Maybe, while dating, some might venture out. But, once they married and settled down, they found everything they wanted and needed right in their little German neighborhood.

The neighborhood had hospitals, schools, grocery stores, movie theaters, banks and restaurants. What else could a person want? A person could be born in the local hospital, live his whole life without having to travel more than a few blocks, then die. And when he died, in Glendale, Queens, he could be buried in one of the many nearby cemeteries.

When I suggest that there were many cemeteries in the area, I mean there were *many*. For instance, within a casual "dog walk" from our apartment, there were at least the following final resting place choices: Mount Olivet, Lutheran (which is one of the places we liked to run), Linden Hill, Mount Lebanon, Mount Carmel, New Union Field, Mount Neboh, Evergreen, St. Johns, Mount Zion, Calvary, and Cypress Hills. All those cemeteries were within a dozen or so blocks.

If that list did not satisfy a person's final wishes, there was always the cremation option.

After scrutinizing maps of the city, I came to the conclusion that it would make a lot of sense to bury people vertically. You could squeeze two or three times the number of bodies into the same real estate—and we all know that real estate in New York is at a premium.

I had another good idea. Why not bury the dead along the railroad tracks? There are, after all, railroad tracks running throughout New York City. And if you stop and think about it, railroad tracks are almost as permanent as cemeteries. It's a simple fact, once you build a railroad, you leave it there. All you would have to do is plant the corpses (vertically, of course), in two or three rows, on each side of the railroad tracks. Noise would not be a concern. You would just have to schedule the funerals according to the train schedule, and those don't change much either.

There would be other benefits, especially for commuters. All you would have to do to pay respects to dear Aunt Hilda would be to select a seat on her side of the train, and when you passed her stone you could remove your hat and observe a moment of silence.

Then, on Memorial Day, you could open the window, and toss a wreath. If you had a little imagination, and a lot of finesse, you could try for a ringer on her stone.

I love New York.

Railroads and cemeteries according to Girl: Okay, here's the deal, we lived smack dab in the middle of at least twenty cemeteries. I am not kidding. There was the Lutheran Cemetery to our north, next to Mount Olivet Cemetery, to our east was St. Johns, to the south was the Cluster of Evergreen, Knollwood Park, Most Holy Trinity, Mount Judah, Union Field, Machpelah, Hungarian, New Union Field, Mount Neboh, Mount Carmel, Cypress Hills and Cypress Hills National, Salem Fields, Shearith, Maimonides, Mount Lebanon and Mount Hope.

Slicing through the silent stillness of the dead were the iron and steel tracks of the Long Island Railroad. Yes, silent cemeteries and rumbling railroads, these two opposites. Had the city planners been around during their inception, they probably would not have placed the two in the same vicinity, even though those noisy freight and passenger trains have always been the lifeblood of the city.

Perhaps it was not by accident, after all, that cemeteries and railroads are so intertwined. It is a simple fact that the dead could never complain.

What was the deal with all of the cemeteries, anyway? Not sure, it didn't really matter. As far as Mike and I were concerned, we liked the fact that there were a lot of cemeteries located near us. We took advantage of the quiet setting they offered for walking our dogs. Once we entered a cemetery, we would unleash the dogs. This worked out most of the time. But, occasionally one of them would spot a squirrel or other small animal, then the hunter in them would be unleashed, like a bat out of ...well, you know.

One of the innate traits of Mister's breed (Norwegian Elkhound) was the uncanny ability to focus on a target. He would block out all else and run. It was virtually impossible to get his attention until his squirrel was out of reach, up a tree and out on a limb. Then, he would choose to find us and transform back into our mild-mannered pet.

Mike and I spent many hours in the cemeteries. The trees were mature, the oaks and maples went through their seasonal changes while the pines elegantly draped the gravestones, protecting and watching over their charges, much like the sentinel in Arlington who guards the Tomb of the Unknown Soldier.

A hushed silence followed us home those nights; it would be a solemn ritual that created within us a sense of awe and compassion for those gone on before us.

The real skinny (according to Boy): I think Evie was more on target than was I. There does seem to be something that attracts us to cemeteries. We both hate funerals, but we tend to gravitate to cemeteries.

When we lived in Philadelphia, we spent hours and hours going through the historical cemeteries. In Glendale, we ran daily in a cemetery. Now, at sixty-five, I still run three days a week in a cemetery. This morning I saw the coolest group of three deer while I was running—in a cemetery.

Vignette 5—Bonnie and Clyde

According to Boy: Evie and I came to be known as "Bonnie and Clyde" after the third time we were convicted of bank robbery. Actually, I think the papers started calling us that after our third prison break. Fortunately, the statute of limitations has expired for our crimes, and leaves us free as birds today.

Of course, I'm joking. Bonnie and Clyde were the names of our neighbors who lived down the street in Glendale. They were not exactly our neighbors, though. More correctly they were Mister's neighbors. Bonnie and Clyde were the St. Bernard puppies that lived two doors down. They always played in the backyard behind their apartment. While they were fenced in, they were always in full view of Mister. And he absolutely loved leaning out our window and "talking" to them. While Bonnie and Clyde did not totally ignore Mister, they were most intrigued with their own backyard. Besides, they were puppies.

They each weighed about fifteen pounds; at least that's what they weighed when they first moved in down the street. I think they gained about one pound a day. Mister was a full-grown Norwegian Elkhound, weighing about forty.

When our neighbors got home in the evening, the first thing they did was to let the puppies out. Mister would be waiting. He would already be at the window, bouncing his front paws on the window sill. When his buddies appeared, he went nuts.

He would not bark—not really. He knew we did not like him to do that. But he could produce the most shrill, high volume whine that a person could imagine. When one of them escaped his mouth, he would immediately turn to see how strongly we disapproved.

"Mister, be quiet!" I would command.

He would then let escape a small whine in protest, turn, leave the window, and come over to me to seek my approval. Then he would go back to the window. Usually, at that point, he would behave.

We took Mister to the cemetery every evening. Our neighbors took their dogs there as well, usually a little earlier in the evening.

If we happened to spot them ahead of us, we would take a detour and enter from the far end of the cemetery. We knew that by the time we had made our way to the near end, our neighbors would be finished walking their dogs.

Sometimes, unfortunately, Mister would find the piles of golden treasure left behind by his well-fed friends. I had to keep a close eye on him, to keep him out of it.

By the time we moved into the Village, the puppies had gained a lot of weight, probably weighing almost a hundred pounds each, on their way to two hundred plus.

I am just glad I did not have to buy the food for those giants.

Bonnie and Clyde according to Girl: I love dogs. These were the two most adorable St. Bernards I had ever laid my eyes on. They were brother and sister from a huge litter. They were only a few weeks old when we first looked out from our kitchen window, and saw them playing in the backyard next door. The row house, with its clothesline and pulleys, often lent itself to a little harmless snooping on our neighbors without seeming too obvious.

Whenever I would hang laundry out on my clothesline, I could not help but stand and watch these huge-pawed happy little guys playing below.

As the weeks passed, we finally got to meet them. We were introduced to Bonnie and Clyde one day in the late fall, when we ran into them on the way to the cemetery. No longer little puppies, They now stood six inches taller than Mister, well on their way to their adult height and weight (which eventually could be three hundred pounds each!).

Bonnie and Clyde were the fluffy coated variety of St. Bernard.

"Won't be long before they can carry their barrel of rescue brandy to lost Alpine skiers," I thought.

One of the other things we noticed from the window, was the deterioration of the backyard. Little by little, it became a toxic waste dump. With two huge dogs, and a postage stamp-sized yard—you get the picture.

I don't remember if Mister came to live with us before or after Bonnie and Clyde came to the neighborhood, however if you got downwind of the yard, you would understand why not everyone should own a St. Bernard.

The real skinny (according to Boy): I think we both remembered the same story here: Big dogs, small yard, lots of poop, and Mister's intrigue. What else is there to say?

Vignette 6—Green silk bedspread

According to Boy: One of the very first things we bought when we moved into the Glendale apartment was a bed. When we got married my mother gave me a hundred dollars (in twenty-dollar bills), and told me to buy a nice set of box springs and a mattress. We did just that. I don't think the used frame was anything to shout about, but the mattress and box springs were new. My mother really liked Evie, and she wanted to make sure Evie had a good bed. That was important to my mother.

The second thing we bought (at least the second new thing) was a green silk bedspread. If I were to describe the color, I think I would call it "pea green." Perhaps there is no such color, but I still think that would be how I would describe it—almost an army green, but shiny.

It was really nice. It was made out of real silk, and it was quite thick. When we crawled under it (I know you're not supposed to crawl under a bedspread—but we did), it was warm and relaxing. And that's one of its attributes that I really liked. It just felt good from underneath. It had enough weight to hold the blanket down close to the body on a cold night.

While I liked the way it looked on the bed, and I liked the way it felt when I crawled under it, my favorite thing about that green silk bedspread was the way it felt to the touch.

Shortly after the acquisition of our new bedspread, we got a dog— Mister. Mister also liked the bedspread. Whenever we were gone, he would jump on the bed and lie on it. That's when I bought "Cheetah." Cheetah was a cheetah pelt (discussed in greater detail in another chapter) that we bought in Greenwich Village. It was a real cheetah hide. The fur was very soft, and the hide underneath was well processed and soft as well. We just tossed Cheetah over the middle of the bedspread, and all was well. Mister liked it, and Cheetah handled a soapy cloth better than did the green silk bedspread.

By the time we were ready to move into the Village (two years later), Mr. Green Silk Bedspread moved into a trash can. We carefully folded it, much as one would fold a tattered American flag in preparation for an honorable disposal; then we tucked it in the bottom of the trash can. We did not want it to share its memories with some homeless guy in the park. It had, after all, done its job admirably for us—it deserved a respectable retirement.

Green silk bedspread according to Girl: My taste in décor was not nearly as developed in 1968 as it is today. I now pull ideas from my sisters, my kids, photography books and the internet. In the sixties, my sisters were just kids; there were no babies, no money for photography books and above all, no Google. It makes me wonder how we ever survived.

The big event was finding the exact, perfect, most wonderful bedspread for our master bedroom. I'm not sure whether or not it's acceptable to call an only bedroom a "master" bedroom, but we did. Mike said the choice of bedspread was mine.

Color was top priority. I wanted it to match his eyes. This was a journey to find the perfect green—perhaps best described as "ocean green."

Ocean green must be distinguished from the aqua blue of the ocean in southern Mexico. Beautiful as that was, it was the wrong color. Of course, the "Finding Nemo" blue water of the poor little fish's delightful adventures was also the wrong color.

I needed the bold, deep, crashing greens of the sea, the colors of the Titanic's ocean, and the strong expressive green of the waves cresting over the shores in Nantucket; that lonely green reflected by the waters teasing the lighthouse at the end of Long Island. The exact dynamic green I was looking for had to match the storm of the century—the color of the deep.

Our quest began near our apartment Glendale, then proceeded to take us through Brooklyn, Queens, and finally to Manhattan. It was in Manhattan, across from the Empire State Building, down the street from the Garden, at the famous Macy's Department Store, that at last I found it.

There it was—expensive, silk, and one of a kind (remember, he did say it was my choice).

We credit carded this wonderful ocean colored addition to our possessions. This was the first time we had purchased something new for our home. It was my perfect storm.

The real skinny (according to Girl): I pretty much had the color down. Mike told the nitty gritty of the bed, fabric and the ultimate demise of the spread. My story could be accurately embedded in his six-paragraph account.

Vignette 7—The day Mister came to live with us

According to Boy: It was a cool October morning. A Saturday morning. The sort of morning made for sleeping in. And that is exactly what my body was doing. Catatonic, in fact. The cause of my condition could be debated. Was it the result of the wine the night before, or the cool October air? Whatever the reason, it seemed doubtful that my mind was going to reach any agreement with my body to engage itself in some sort of conscious movement.

"Mike, wake up," Evie pleaded. I could hear her only as I incorporated her voice into my dream. I have no idea what I was dreaming, but she had suddenly become part of it.

"We've got to pick up our dog."

That three-letter word did not compute. "Dog?" I queried struggling to wake up. "Dog?"

I opened my eyes to the light, but only for a moment. The sun's light illuminating our almost white curtains was more than I could bear. The pain was centered mostly behind my right eye. That's where it always hurt the morning after.

"Oh," I moaned. "I've got a killer headache."

The word "dog" was starting to make sense. Then I remembered. We had agreed to provide a home to a dog. Charlie, our most-wonderful landlord, had asked us to adopt his friend's dog. I wasn't terribly excited about the prospect of being a dad to a dog, but Charlie had been so very helpful to us. When we moved into our Glendale apartment, which was located over where Charlie and his family lived, we did not even have a bed. He called around and found us a really nice one. He and his family were just terrific. He had explained to us that his friend was moving into an apartment, and that his new landlord would not allow pets. How could I refuse?

Besides that, Evie was ecstatic about having a dog. "Must have been her maternal instincts kicking in," I concluded.

Lying there, still half asleep, and severely hung over, I muttered, "What the heck is a Norwegian Elkhound, anyway?" Being that this was the late 60s (BG—before Google), we really had no good way to investigate.

"I really don't know much about them, but Charlie said that they're really cool," Evie said in her most excited and convincing tone. "Charlie said that the dog's name was 'Mista'. That's Brooklynese for 'Mister.'"

"So, I suppose that means that it's a male. But that does not tell me much about what the dog looks like, or the temperament of the breed. Is it a large dog?"

"No, Charlie said he really would not like us to get a large dog, but that Mista would be okay," Evie explained.

"Wait a minute. Had you asked him if we could have a dog, or did he ask you if we would be willing to take this dog? You know, which came first, the chicken or the egg?"

"Well, it's kind of complicated," Evie replied.

"What do you mean?" I asked, squinting one painfully bloodshot eye open in her direction.

"It was kinda mutual," she responded. "I asked him if he would ever entertain the notion of a renter having a pet, like a cat. And he said he would check with his wife and see what she thought. He really thought that a cat would not be acceptable to his wife, because they had once had a cat themselves, and she got rid of it after it stunk up their house. But she might consider a dog—a small dog."

"Okay, that explains a lot," I said, now fully awake. I had found it difficult to understand why any landlord would ask his tenant to please accept and house a pet, even a 'small' dog, in a newly-refurbished apartment directly over his own residence.

Charlie was branch manager of a Brooklyn bank. And the friend whose dog needed a home was his assistant manager. Charlie was a genuinely nice person. So was his family. Charlie had even arranged for Evie to take a job as a teller at his bank. That was a huge help. Charlie was the type of person who truly tried to take care of people, to make all those around him a little more comfortable. Of course, it was helpful to his cause to have his tenants employed. But he liked us, and wanted to make sure Evie had a good, clean and safe job. He was like that. So, when his assistant asked him if he could help him find a good home for "Mista" (spelled "Mister"), Charlie immediately took personal responsibility for giving the task his best effort, even if it meant allowing (encouraging in fact) his tenant to take the animal. I doubt that Charlie had any better idea what a Norwegian Elkhound looked like than did we.

"We promised to be there by ten, and I have no idea how long it will take to get there," Evie said in her most coaxing and pleading voice. "It's nine now. We should leave in the next fifteen, I think."

"Do we have a map?" I asked.

"No, but Charlie gave me directions. He said we should be able get there in about a half an hour, with Saturday morning traffic. So, if we allow ourselves forty minutes, we can make a few wrong turns, and still be okay," Evie grinned.

"I would still like to know what a Norwegian Elkhound looks like,"

I said, putting one and then the other foot on the floor, and sitting up—finally. Man, what a headache.

"Charlie told me Mista was a small dog, and that he even went to obedience school," Evie said, trying to encourage me.

I pictured Mista as being a mixture of Collie and Poodle. What did I know? I had never heard of Norwegian Elkhounds. Maybe it was not even a real breed of dog. Maybe Charlie's friend had just made up the appellation to help get rid of his unwanted dog. What were we getting ourselves into?

The day Mister came to live with us according to Girl: Oh my gosh, my heart was beating so fast I could hardly contain myself. Yes, this was the day I was so anxiously awaiting. We had made all of the arrangements with the landlord, the owner and the transportation details, and we had a map. We would be on our way in the next few hours to get him, and I was excited. How could Mike sleep in on a day like this, he would be my very first, no-one-could-take-him away-from-me dog, and he was joining our family as our very special pet. He would greet me with tail wagging and lots of sloppy dog licks and kisses. He would be so very happy to share our lives, I just knew it. Mike and I would sort of now be a real family with a real, honest to goodness living and breathing puppy.

I think I am actually a very big dog person. I have, however, had many disappointments along the way (at least in that area).

When I was eleven, my family was still living in a tiny apartment on McReynolds Street. I already had three siblings—Tom (9), Tim (7), and the new baby, Liz. I was so thankful when Liz was born, I had been praying for a sister for a very long time. With the appearance of Liz, I was optimistic that things were going to change—all I now needed was a dog

That's when "Blackie," the stray, wandered into our yard. I came home from school one afternoon, and there he was. He was a very scraggly dog, but very loveable. He had black wavy hair (filled with burrs), and was very skinny. Nancy, my best friend in the world, helped me scour the alley behind our home for important stuff to welcome my new dog. We found a lot of treasures there—old dog dishes from other people's garbage, old refrigerator or stove boxes (we used them to make Blackie a shelter (which was fine until it rained), stinky blankets, and lots of things for him to chew on.

I could not wait to get home from school each night. I would brush Blackie, pet him, get him his water and leftovers from dinner. He devoured the best of those pork chop bones, green beans and slightly stale mashed potatoes. Blackie was putting on weight and was becoming a very happy dog. Yes, Blackie stuck around.

As the weeks progressed, Mom and Dad found our little home bursting at the seams, and they made an offer on a huge two-story home across town. Before I knew what was happening, Dad loaded us, our clothes, and all our basic furnishings into our "wood on the side" station wagon, and away we moved to the other side of town—without Blackie.

Dad was not ready to be the official owner of another mouth to feed. I cried, and said goodbye to my Blackie. Nancy promised to raise him right.

"Mike, get up, let's go get the dog." It was so very important to me. "No, let's not stop to get breakfast. No coffee for me, I am packed and ready to hit the road. We can't keep our new dog waiting."

My second attempt at adopting a dog was in the spring of my twelfth year, while I was visiting my cousins. They were four rowdy boys with a collie. This collie had puppies six weeks earlier, and I was getting a fluffy little cute butterball of a puppy—Mom and Dad had already said it was okay.

I found a box and a blanket. I could not put the little girl pup down, she was so soft and cuddly. She spent that Sunday afternoon in my lap mostly sleeping and sipping a bit of milk from a doll bottle. We were sitting together in the sunlight by the west windows in the dining room, when on the buffet, the mean, ugly, black phone rang. It was the ring of death. My aunt was on the phone, demanding the return of my puppy. She said my puppy had earlier been promised to one of her friends who lived on a farm. My heart was broken.

From that time on, until Mike and I married, I had accepted my "dogless" fate. But now, things were going to be different.

Finally, Mike and I were ready to hit the road. It was going to be a long drive, all the way out on Long Island. Long Island is about thirty-five miles long and six miles wide. My map took us to the east end of the island. Our Glendale apartment was located on the west end of Long Island. Lucky for us, we still had our fast Mustang.

We were told "Mister" was a medium-sized dog, and that he had attended dog school. "He must be a very well-behaved dog," I recall thinking.

The owners had to find a home for him quickly. They just had a new baby. While Mister was a great dog, they felt they had to focus on the newborn. It was so good of Charlie, our landlord, to fill us in on the details.

We drove up to the big house and property, and around to a huge patio in the back. A very sweet couple came out to greet us. All four of us shared the biggest smiles.

Then, I saw him, coming around a corner. He was beautiful. The moment our brown eyes met, I knew it was true love. He was exactly what I wanted—well, maybe a bit bigger that I had originally expected, but he was very happy to meet us.

His coat (fur) was black, gray and white, he had a tail that curled up over his back. It was wagging like crazy. He stood up on his tippy puppy toes to greet us, sort of jumping up and down, as if telling us he was ready to go.

His "parents" told us all the details we needed to know about how to take care of their beloved baby. They explained that he had received all of his shots, and that he graduated with honors from his obedience school.

Little did I realize at the time that obedience school only meant he knew how to sit in a corner and drool for food, rather than begging out loud for pizza leftovers.

I was ready to be a pet owner, I learned how to give a Mister a bath, walk, and feed him. One of things his original parents told us was that Mister was on a special diet—he ate only a very expensive dog food. The product they suggested was very expensive, and could be purchased in only a few stores. Nevertheless, that's what we bought for him.

That was great, as far as I was concerned. Soon the three of us climbed into that little Mustang and headed back toward the city. And he (my sweet Mister dog) was really coming back with us. I was ready.

Yes, it was truly the perfect day. The sun was shining, the grass was green and we had our first dog. Mister would be a part of our New York life for years to come.

The real skinny (according to Boy): I really can't believe that we agreed on almost everything having to do with the new member of the family. I did not actually remember who had suggested we adopt Mister. But, apparently it was our landlord. It seems strange that a landlord would find a dog for a tenant. Charlie and his family were truly wonderful people. I do not think that I have ever met a family cooler than were they.

I also was not sure about Evie having to wake me up. It was, however logical. The only day that we would have time to drive out into the country would be a Saturday morning. So that part of the story just figured.

Again, I do not remember the details.

I do remember just how excited Evie was about this whole thing. I think that is obvious in both accounts.

Vignette 8—New York Mounted Police

According to Boy: One of the great charms of New York is the horses in Central Park. All by itself Central Park is pretty amazing. Its size alone is staggering—eight hundred forty-three acres, almost a third of which is forest. Today it boasts twenty-three leash-free pet friendly zones; I think the whole park might have been leash-free back in 1968, but I don't remember for sure. Still, what I remember best about the park are the horses. And, of course, the resulting piles of horse manure.

My gut tells me that the New York Mounted Police division is somehow protected by a union. Otherwise, they would long ago have been replaced by cops on bicycles in the summer, and in Jeeps in the winter. There is just simply no way that this practice can be justified financially. All leading me to think there must be a union behind it.

Now there are some practical benefits of having a cop on a horse, as opposed to a cop on a bike. For instance, I have never been able to think of cops on bikes as any more than boy scouts in short pants trying to earn a merit badge. Granted, they carry guns just like real cops, but they just don't look like real cops.

But, a cop on horseback is a very imposing sight. For one thing, he has a thousand pounds of muscle beneath him. And I don't remember the mounted cops wearing short pants. I could be wrong, but I seem to recall them sporting long riding pants tucked inside high riding boots.

If you just stop and think about it, which would instill more fear in a bad guy—a boy scout on a two-wheeler, or an eight-foot tall helmeted John Wayne with a gun? Granted, both of them could kill you, but John Wayne would stand a better chance of getting your attention without deadly force.

Also, the mounted cops were extremely effective at crowd control, an attribute that came in very handy during the 1960s. They were easy to spot from a distance. This allowed the less inspired troublemakers to split, leaving only the hard core to deal with.

Another group of horses common to the park were the ones used to pull the little carriages for tourists. I am really surprised that they are still there. As I write this, Evie and I are again visiting New York, and the horse-drawn carriages are still prevalent in the park. If you think about it, don't you wonder why PETA doesn't bomb someplace to put an end to this mistreatment of animals? I think I even saw one of the carriage drivers wearing a leather jacket, and I know I spotted a woman in a real fur coat riding behind him. Where are those well-intentioned terrorists when you need them?

Needless to say, Evie and I never rented one of those carriages. But it was not because of political reasons. Personally, if it can't do wheelies, or lay a patch in three gears, I'm not much interested. And as for Evie, she never suggested we do it. I think she would rather ride on the horse, than watch it dump its load. That part of the deal was never particularly intriguing to me either.

Evie and I did spend a considerable amount of time walking in Central Park. And we found one of the biggest challenges was to avoid stepping in fertilizer. They just don't make pooper-scoopers that big. And it is virtually impossible to curb a horse. Nevertheless, we both still loved the sight (if not the smell) of the horses in Central Park.

New York Mounted Police according to Girl: The drums shook the hotel, we were not sure if it was thunder accompanying the rain, or perhaps the Blue Angels performing a drive-by, but upon entering the bathroom, with the tiny window (which was above the larger double-hung window) barely opened, we heard the faint horns of the brass. "Must be a parade," I thought. On this rainy, windy day, we just had to check it out. We ran out of our room, and jumped on the elevator. I mentioned the drums to a British mom with her two girls. They were also in search of the parade. We passed cold windblown people, girls in colorful rain boots, umbrellas turned inside out from the stiff forty-mile-per-hour gusts. A young man dashed past us, against the light, with a chubby little cop at his heels. The streets were still filled, but the parade must have ended. The music had stopped.

I guarantee there will be another, because New York loves parades.

I guarantee the streets will be full again.

I guarantee the shops will be open.

I guarantee the police will be there, running down the bad guys.

I guarantee the horses will be plentiful in Central Park, pulling carriages, in the rain, in the snow, and on miserably hot or icy cold days. The passengers will be offered warm wool blankets and a paper bag full of roasted chestnuts.

I guarantee that there will be mounted police with big black boots. They will command their steeds like storm troopers. Just as Darth Vader once said, "The Empire has a legion of loyal soldiers that are in endless supply." He might have been describing the Galactic Empire; but to me, it fits New York.

We were celebrating the anniversary of the unveiling of the Statue of Liberty. On this date in 1886, she was dedicated by President Grover Cleveland. We surmised correctly that this might have been the reason for the parade.

"Give me your tired, your poor, your huddled masses yearning to breathe free, the wretched refuse of your teeming shore. Send these, the homeless, tempest-tossed to me, I lift my lamp beside the golden door!"

The real skinny (according to Boy): After reading Evie's chapter, I feel just a little guilty. More than ever, I get the feeling that she would like to have gone on one of those carriage rides. Maybe I'll offer on one of our New York trips in the next year. It is not especially inviting to me, but I'm sure it could be fun. And one more thing: This chapter was supposed to be exclusively about the mounted police, not New York horses in general. I should learn to read the instructions. That malady just might reside in my genes.

Vignette 9—Coney Island and Rockaways' Playland

According to Boy: There are simply some things I recall better than does Evie. She doesn't remember Rockaways' Playland. I think she might not even think she was ever there—but she was. She went there with me in 1968, or possibly 1969.

The amusement park was located in Queens. We lived in Queens from 1968 to 1970. One of the reasons (perhaps the only reason) I remember so vividly our visit to the park is that it was on this memorable trip that she and I rode the roller coaster. It was, in fact, the last roller coaster I ever rode.

I think the coaster we rode was the well-known "Cinerama Coaster," made famous by the 1950s movie "This is Cinerama." In its day, the Cinerama was quite the roller coaster. The track was 3000 feet long and 70 feet high—not terribly impressive by today's standard, but pretty cool "back in the day." That ride was the first time she and I ever rode on a roller coaster together, and the last for both of us. The reason being, it nearly killed me.

I never was a great fan of roller coasters. Prior to that day, I think I may have ridden on one three or four times in my life, and each time I got sick during the ride, or immediately after getting off. This time I thought I would try something different—I closed my eyes.

For the first few minutes, my new strategy worked. I made it to the top without getting ill. I thought I had figured it out. Then, when the bottom fell out, my stomach rose into my throat. Still, I kept my eyes closed, and my mouth as well.

It almost seemed as though I was going to make it. I had let my mind drift, and I was relaxing. However, when the car suddenly banked sharply and turned to the right, my neck snapped. I had pulled a muscle and tweaked a nerve. One arm went numb. I immediately opened my eyes. The pain in my neck and head was excruciating. I grabbed my head between my hands to steady it, and I silently prayed for an end to this ordeal.

I spent the remainder of this "fun" trip sick to my stomach, and wearing my head more than a little like Ed Sullivan wore his. When I wanted to check something out on my right or left, I would turn my whole body in that direction. My stomach did not begin to feel better until well into the next day, and my neck took several more weeks to repair.

As far as Coney Island is concerned, all I remember about it are the hot dogs. Coney Island is located in Brooklyn, and it competed with Rockaways' Playland. Evie and I did go to Coney Island on one of our adventures, but I do not remember much about it.

I do remember that I had a "Coney Island hot dog" just before I got on the roller coaster at Rockaways' Playland. Probably that was my downfall.

The Queen's park closed in the mid 1980s. I understand that Coney Island is now a substantially run down area of Brooklyn. We have been back to New York dozens of times after we moved out of the city, but we have never been tempted to check out the amusement parks.

Coney Island and Rockaways' Playland according to Girl: "Conyne Eylandt," meaning Rabbit Island, on the New Netherland map of 1639. Somehow, we missed it. It was like the "Brooklynites," who never crossed the river into Manhattan, and the Bronx residents never venturing east to Long Island.

Were we becoming like them—trapped in our own world of "places we visited?" No, I do not really believe that. We did hit the museums, art galleries, ball games, and beaches. We saw the city from the top of the Empire State Building, and even visited the rocky shores of the Hampton's. Our weekends took us to the wilderness and forested Catskills, as well as south to the Staten Island Ferry.

So, what happened to Coney Island? It was an amusement park with all of the glamour of lights, rides, and hot dogs. It was a place where I could easily find myself becoming very queasy. I could get out of control. Those wonderful Coney Island Dogs, filled with chili, sauerkraut, and mustard. (By the way, some have suggested that the Coney Island Dogs actually originated in Michigan!) Also available at amusement parks were red crunchy and crispy candy apples, pink and blue cotton candy, popcorn and lemonade. Top that off with a ride on a 150 foot ferris wheel, and a huge roller coaster with an eighty-five foot drop, and you could easily find me turning many shades of green.

But that was not why we missed it. We always said, "we should go there. We could spend a Saturday. Let's take company there." But we never did.

How could anything be as grand as Rockefeller Center? Or as amazing as the Guggenheim? Could anything compare with the elevator ride up the Empire State Building? How could I forget the lights of Times Square? Or what could top the importance of the Lady?

Yes, Michigan had Coney Island Dogs, Ferris wheels and roller coasters. Mike and I found our weekends filled with the wonder of the most amazing city in the world. We drank deeply from its history and wanted to take a part of it with us when it was time to leave.

So, we walked. We splashed in its fountains, we ran through Central Park, we kissed on the subways and hugged on its streets. Falling more in love with each other and committing to yes, someday visit Coney Island. Perhaps we will, someday.

The real skinny (according to Boy): Evie and I have been to Las Vegas a couple of dozen times through the years. Whenever we go, we either do not gamble at all, or I might drop $20 in a machine while waiting for her. We do not gamble. However, concerning the Coney Island Amusement, I would make an exception. I am positive that we went there. I vividly recall hurting my neck there. I would bet the whole farm on that.

Vignette 10—The Garbage Strike of 1968

According to Boy: I always liked to celebrate Evie's birthday. On February 2, 1968, Local 831 of New York's Uniformed Sanitationmen's Association decided to start the celebration a little early—their president, John DeLury, ordered the workers off the job. They remained on strike for over a week, leaving the trash of eight million people to pile up on sidewalks and in alleys to the point that it was almost impossible to get around the city.

Of course, had the strike occurred in the summer, it would have been worse. But it was still bad enough. I recall walking along the sidewalk, holding a cloth over my face to block the smell, and the dirt. Not only was the trash not being collected, the streets were not being swept, and the prevailing winter winds that whistled through the streets carried with it tons of dust and grime. All the small shops and bars deposited the sweepings from their floors into the street just off the curbs. It then simply got redistributed down the block.

Restaurants still put their waste, organic garbage included, onto the sidewalk in anticipation of an expeditious end to the strike. Dogs, cats and rats feasted on the garbage, dragging pieces into the street, and fighting over them there. The stench was unbelievable. The whole city was transformed into a scene reminiscent of a Mad Max movie.

I recall coming back into my apartment and running right for the bathroom to brush my teeth. I swear I could taste the rotten garbage. I would then shower and put on a change of clothes.

There grew out of this strike a number of stories about how enterprising residents disposed of their trash. My favorite was of a man who every morning carefully packed his trash in a neat box, and gift wrapped it. Then he would leave it on his car seat, with his door unlocked. According to this "urban legend," he never failed to have his trash "stolen."

We were not so clever. We just filled some big trash bags, sealed them well, and stashed them in the corner of the kitchen for the duration.

I do think we went out to eat every night, until the strike was settled. That held down trash production.

The garbage strike of 1968 according to Girl: It was the summer of 1968. Mike was a pro at handling the big city life; I was much less acquainted with all of the joys and noise of the city.

There was the screech of steel brakes on steel wheels as the subway stopped for its passengers of the hour.

There were the tireless horns of the taxi's encouraging the traffic to move.

There was the urine smell that drifted up from the private corners of the dark buildings—those places most familiar to the homeless (and bar patrons after closing time) needing to relieve themselves.

And, last but not least, there was the amazing garbage strike.

This was not your ordinary *trash got missed* day. This was serious, twelve foot high piles of trash.

Talk about stench, rats, roaches—the city had it all in 1968. You learned how to hold your breath when walking by the black plastic mountains of trash.

Five days into the strike, on the sixth of February, 1968, 50,000 tons of uncollected garbage had accumulated. Uniformed Sanitationmen's Association President John DeLury announced that while he would send his men out without pay to pick up the garbage at the seventy-one city hospitals, they would not attend to the 10,000 tons that were added daily in the city. For that, he went to jail.

As far as union leaders were concerned, every union chief was expected to welcome imprisonment—it was the only acceptable way to prove your worth in that position.

Sanitation men received salaries ranging from $6,424 to $7,956. DeLury wanted a $600 hike. The city was offering $400.

Okay, it was not all bad. We found a table and a few chairs out in the street. People would throw away some pretty good stuff. We knew with a little glue, some nails and a hammer, most discarded furniture was still usable. We recycled. We did our share to help the city during the crisis and I knew that. In retrospect, I can look back and see the good. I still love the city with its noises, smells, traffic and congestion. Like Neil Simon, I truly can see comedy and creativity come out of the pavement and architecture of the city.

Viva New York!

The real skinny (according to Boy): My gosh, Evie really got into this one. I think we were on the same page—she just wrote in the margins.

Vignette 11—Folded, with heavy starch

According to Boy: "Shaken, not stirred." Or was it "stirred, not shaken?"

However it was that Bond ordered his martinis, I'm not really sure. I think it was "shaken, not stirred." But I am sure about my shirts: "Folded, with heavy starch." Today I don't have to say a thing when I bring my shirts to the laundry. "Mr. Carrier, we know how you like them—you're on our computer."

Back in 1968, I wasn't on anyone's computer. So I always had to tell the laundry clerk just how I wanted them done. Too many times I would be disappointed. Either they would fail to use adequate starch, or they would put them on hangers. In either instance, I would refuse them. I could tell immediately by just touching the shirt if they had forgotten the starch. I always kept a couple spares just in case they screwed up. I think that happened almost ten percent of the time.

Why did I like them folded? Simple. I liked what they felt like when I unfolded them and put them on. They were crisp and clean. I even liked the creases where they were folded.

I liked the heavy starch for a few reasons. First of all, it made them look new. It held the folds in for the entire day. Wearing a shirt like that made me feel dressed up, and good about myself. I also liked the heavy starch because of what it did to the collar. Even though it sometimes irritated my neck, the stiff collar looked sharp with a nice tie. Another reason I liked having my shirts starched heavy was so that I could wear them twice. And I sure did that. I would unbutton the top few buttons, and slip the shirt over my head when I came home. The next day I would slip it back on, and it would still look good. The creases were still there.

Finally, I liked the crisp appearance of a well-starched shirt because Evie liked it that way. She frequently would grab one of my worn-once shirts, and slip it on to run around our apartment. The shirts were long enough so that she would not have to wear anything under it.

Occasionally I would forget that she had worn one of my shirts, and I would slip it on the next morning. I would not realize right away that something was wrong. But as soon as I got to work, and sat down, I would start sensing her Estee Lauder Youth Dew perfume. I found it exhilarating, but also a little embarrassing.

There is an additional aspect to this story that I have never before shared with Evie. I never told her about it because I was not proud of it. It was one of those things that I just put out of my mind, and only now, with the writing of this chapter, did I remember it.

The history of my being so fussy about my shirts extended all the way back to high school. I was never happy with the way my shirts looked coming off the clothesline. So, early on, I started doing my own shirts. I starched them and ironed them. My mom was not excited about taking "special orders," but she had no problem teaching me.

Then, as an undergraduate, I started my own little business. I had absolutely no money for pop and pizzas, so I started washing, starching, ironing, and folding the dress shirts for the upper classmen. I think I charged a quarter a shirt. Not much, but it provided change for the student union.

By my second year, I got a job writing catalog ads and editing articles for a local publishing company. So I no longer farmed out my domestic services. However, I continued doing my own shirts—heavy starch, and always folded.

Folded, with heavy starch according to Girl: It was one of those sunny days where the colors of summer crash and bump into the autumn hues; the air starts smelling of falling leaves, and the breezes become cooler and more refreshing. It is a pure joy to take it all in, to fill your lungs and close your eyes. The tips of the maples began to show the softer greens and yellows, moment by moment, loosing leaves to the wind.

I was walking home from the bus stop, happy to feel the dancing, moving air on my face. My pace quickened the closer I got. Finally arriving, I ran up the first set of concrete steps, taking two at a time, landed on the gray-painted porch, and burst through the front door. I reminded myself of Tigger from Winnie the Poo as I ran up the stairway to our first apartment.

Thank goodness Mrs. Robinson was not outside sweeping the steps or sidewalk. If she were, I would have to stop, tell her about my day, tell her about the bus ride, about the stories from work, and then politely excuse myself to head up the steps to Mike. She was a doll, and I really liked her, but this day I was in a hurry.

Mike generally tried to get something started for dinner, if he made it home in time. I was famished. We ate a lot of chicken and rice. Someone had given me the recipe for it (along with a casserole dish) at my wedding shower. It was soooo yummy with dried onion soup and mushroom soup. It lasted three days, and was a convenient way to cook. I could almost smell it from the bus stop, I had been thinking about it for an hour.

As I opened the door and kicked off my shoes, I looked around for him, but he was not there. Dinner had not been started. The apartment was small, so I could quickly look through all three rooms. There was no

Mike, and there were no notes on the fridge or on the counter.

"He must have had to stay after school; perhaps to get a project going for one of his classes," I surmised.

Super sleuth that I was, I continued to look around and found our laundry basket was missing about half of the items.

"Were they stolen? Did the crooks leave fingerprints? What all did they take?"

All of my dirty clothes and our towels were still in the basket. "That's curious," I thought. Then I discovered that all of Mike's dress shirts were gone.

"He is really going to be upset. . . . No, wait, perhaps he was kidnapped, perhaps the intruder tied him with a rope, grabbed some shirts and thinks that because I work at the bank, they might be able to get some ransom money from me.

Should I call the police?" I thought about this for a moment. "Not a good idea. I am sure they would hurt or even kill him if the police became involved. Let me think about this some more.

"I know there must be a weapon or two around here. I could possibly defend myself with a baseball bat. We had a few of them. Or my pink rolling pin."

I was ready for that ransom phone call. I sat at the kitchen table on our chrome-legged chairs with the fake marble plastic cushions that went perfectly with the fake marble table top.

"Could I get the money? How much would they want? Where would I meet them? Perhaps in a cemetery—we had plenty of them around. Oh, maybe under the viaduct. Just let them keep Mike alive."

I almost started chewing a nail, and I never chewed nails.

"I think I'm gonna need proof of life!"

I was getting a migraine. I needed a water and aspirin. As I was heading down the hall to the bathroom, not quite knowing if I was going to throw up, Mike walked in.

I screamed, "Oh my gosh, are you okay? Did they hurt you? Just so you know, I was going to meet their demands."

He said, "What are you talking about?"

I told him about the kidnapping. I was shaking and visibly upset.

He told me he had just taken his shirts to the laundry. He then suggested that maybe we should eat at the Glendale Diner that night.

"Okay," I responded immediately. "That sounds good to me. I'm hungry."

I quickly changed into my jeans and we had dinner out.

It's funny how those winds blow.

The real skinny (according to Girl): Positively from my view a story I wrote from an active imagination on this one. Mike was following the actual events of his shirts, while I fabricated a plot of a potential Perry Mason episode. I still like it.

Vignette 12—Tom discovers the Blimpie sub

According to Boy: On April 4, 1964, three young men opened a submarine sandwich store in Hoboken, New Jersey. They did it with a lot of desire and energy, but with only the $2000 that they had coaxed out of a friend (promising to pay him back with fifteen percent of the net profits). At closing time on that first day, they had sold $295 worth of submarine sandwiches.

That means they recouped over ten percent of their original investment, on that first day alone. Wow, what an investment their friend had made! That little sub shop in Hoboken was the first Blimpie restaurant. Today, Blimpie restaurants have become a multi-billion dollar national phenomenon.

It was only four years later, 1968, that Evie and I introduced her father (Tom) to a Blimpie sub. He was more than fascinated. He talked about it during his entire visit. If I did nothing else in my life to lift his spirit, and to help make him think that perhaps his oldest daughter actually might have made a half-decent choice (me), it was taking him through the door at Blimpie's.

Evie and I had discovered the restaurant only a few months earlier. We loved it because you could basically build your own sandwich. You would tell them what you wanted on it, and they would build it for you. The meat always got sliced fresh, and immediately laid on your creation.

Some called the Blimpie sub a "salad in a sandwich." That was a pretty accurate description. At the end of the line you could choose from any number of salad dressings to finish it off. On Tom's first time through, he was right behind me. His eyes were huge. "Mike, what's that?" he must have asked half a dozen times.

He picked up a shaker, and read the label: "Ore-gan-o, what's that?"

"Yeah, you're gonna want some of that. It's 'Oregano,'" I said.

When he got to the dressings, he picked up each of them and read the labels. I am not positive, but I would bet that he was going through the line with his Camel hanging out of the corner of his mouth, and his eyes squinting from the smoke. There was probably an ash about an inch long looking like it was about to fall off.

Evie and I always split a sandwich. I do not remember if he split one with Evie's Mom or not. But I suspect that he had his own—after all, *he* had built it. And Bea did have a mind of her own.

The total conversation at the table that day, and for much of the rest of his visit, was about the Blimpie sub. "We need one of those restaurants in Grand Rapids," he said several times.

The next day, Tom wanted another Blimpie. I think we probably went back for another. Why not? After all, he was the guest.

Of all the people I have ever known, Evie's Dad is on my very short list of favorites. He never talked much, but when he did, you wanted to listen. His demeanor and character commanded my respect, even though I never heard him raise his voice, or make any demands. He was simply a person you wanted to please. I am very happy to have played a part in introducing him to the Blimpie sub.

Dang—I'm starting to get hungry!

Tom discovers the Blimpie sub according to Girl: We would get the Blimpie Best. It involved perhaps the most labor intensive sandwich one could order from any fast food menu in the city.

The young man behind the counter (I think it may have been Tony, maybe Peter, or perhaps Angelo) would take each ingredient you selected, slice it thinly, and place it in your sandwich—all with the expertise of an experienced bartender. He would start with the meats—ham, beef, hard salami, the choices were numerous. After the meats, he would put on your choice of cheeses, lettuce, onions and tomato. Finally, the application of the crème de la crème—a sprinkle of oil, oregano and vinegar.

So, when my parents came to town, we wanted them to experience one of our favorite places to go. We jumped on the train, headed into the city and took them to see the boys from Jersey. The long line was not a problem, because it gave my wide-eyed family time to choose what they wanted on their warm fresh bread.

Dad watched carefully. He was not into new palette adventures. I wasn't sure if this would go over. This was something that a meat and mashed potatoes man could find a bit offensive. I crossed my fingers. We had not thought of a "Plan B" for lunch that day.

As Dad observed the creation of his sandwich through the curved glass, I watched him. He was standing there in line, cigarette hanging from his mouth. He was in obvious awe as the latex-gloved hands of the master sandwich maker pressed a block of ham against the huge stainless steel slicer, then placed the finely cut slices on a scale (to be certain he had the exact amount). Finally, the creator carefully placed them on the freshly sliced bread..

Order was important. Dad was fascinated with the process. The red-peppered cappicola was next. Then huge slices of black peppered prosciuttini, provolone and toppings—it was a work of art.

We were extra hungry that day. We had spent hours and lots of energy walking around the city. As we opened the paper holding our dinner sub,

I held my breath.

Does he like it?

I couldn't bear to look. Perhaps . . . So, I peeked.

He *loved* it.

Success.

We heard about Blimpies for years afterward.

Every time we visited Grand Rapids, he would sit there at the head of the chrome and Formica kitchen table, he would look up over the top of the Grand Rapids Press, tilt his head to keep the smoke out of his eyes, and he would ask, "Do they still have that Blimpie place in the city?"

"Man, it was good!"

The real skinny (according to Girl): Mike and I were pretty much in agreement with the story on the sub. Dad didn't talk much about his trip to New York; however, I distinctly remember his comments on the "Blimpie Best." As time passed and he developed cancer, he was so very thin and in lots of pain, but his eyes would light up when we talked about that Manhattan sub shop, it had become one of his fondest memories.

Those were the days, my friend—
We thought they'd never end.

Made in the USA
Monee, IL
03 May 2025

16770369R00036